CONTENTS

CONTENTS

ACKNOWLEDGMENTS

THANKS to Adrienne, Pam, Andrea, and
Charlotte—the best teachers I have had.

To Henry Holmes, who really taught me to bob,
weave, and counterpunch; and to Bonnie Blasich,
who told me where the buck stops.

To Barney Oldfield, my ghost.

To Dr. Robert Schuller, who, when I was afraid,
pushed me off the stool into the fight of my life.

To my wife, Joan, for love I never knew existed
in this world.

And thank you, Jesus.

TO ALL MY FRIENDS AND FAMILY
at the Church of the Lord Jesus Christ in Houston,
Texas: For more than twenty years, they have
come to church trusting that I would never bring
my problems with me to the pulpit and that I
would try to find answers to help all of us with our
day-to-day grind in life.

AND TO ALL THE MOMS who have
never been ashamed of those of us who were your
children.

SIMON & SCHUSTER

Rockefeller Center

1230 Avenue of the Americas

New York, NY 10020

SIMON & SCHUSTER and colophon are registered

trademarks of Simon & Schuster, Inc.

For information about special discounts for bulk purchases,

please contact Simon & Schuster Special Sales:

1-800-456-6798 or business@simonandschuster.com

Designed by Bonni Leon Berman

Manufactured in the United States of America

10   9   8   7   6   5   4   3   2   1

Library of Congress Cataloging-in-Publication Data

is available.

ISBN   0-7432-2499-X

(Photo credits appear on page 126.)

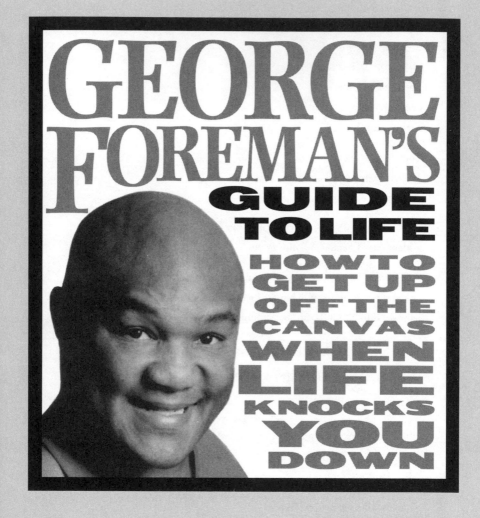

GEORGE FOREMAN'S
GUIDE TO LIFE

HOW TO GET UP OFF THE CANVAS WHEN LIFE KNOCKS YOU DOWN

GEORGE FOREMAN

with Linda Kulman

SIMON & SCHUSTER
New York London Toronto Sydney Singapore

ALSO BY GEORGE FOREMAN

By George: The Autobiography of George Foreman
(with Joel Engel)

George Foreman's Big Book of Grilling, Barbecue, and Rotisserie
(with Barbara Witt)

George Foreman's Knock-Out-the-Fat Barbecue and Grilling Cookbook
(with Cherie Calbom)

INTRODUCTION

THERE'S HARDLY a single lesson I've learned in life that didn't come the hard way. So I know that life can sometimes seem like a big hole, and that you have to be pulled up out of it from time to time. But I also know you *can* pull yourself out. I say this as someone who read his first whole books at the age of sixteen; who was married and divorced four times and found the fifth time to be the charm; who's the oldest person ever to hold the heavyweight boxing title. I know from experience that you should never give up on yourself or others, no matter what. Everyone in life goes through a hard time sometime, but you can't let that define who you are. What defines you is how you come back from those troubles and what you find in life to smile about.

I grew up the fifth of seven children in the toughest neighborhood in Houston, and I didn't have a lot to look forward to in life. At least I didn't *think* I did. I was hungry all the time; I dropped out of school in the eighth grade; I relied on my size and my fists to make my way. I became the world heavyweight champion against Joe Frazier in 1973, only to lose the title I'd worked so hard for a year later in my fight against Muhammad Ali. Imagine losing everything you think matters to you in ten seconds. For a long time in my life, I was so full of rage, people couldn't wait to get out of my way—just like when you see a Doberman pinscher and cross to the other side of the street.

I see a lot of tough guys come into the George Foreman Youth and Community Center in Houston who remind me of myself when I was a teenager. Just like my old friend

The new heavyweight Olympic boxing champ in the 1968 Olympics in Mexico City. The guy to my far left is my first coach from the Job Corps, Charles "Doc" Broadus.

The George Foreman Youth and Community Center in Houston sponsors a camp every summer where all of the kids are given pointers about health and nutrition as well as a grill.

and boxing coach in California, Charles "Doc" Broadus, did with me, I always put them in the ring against the smallest guy there who knows how to box. The big guy comes out all bluster and swinging this way and that. And the little guy doesn't even hit him, he just moves out of the way until after a while, the big guy is completely out of breath. That's usually about the time he realizes that the smaller guy could have killed him with a few well-placed jabs and that it's *how* you fight that counts.

This book is about fighting smart for all the things that

really matter in life: yourself, your relationships, and your kids. I have done some crying while doing this book. I have gotten some old bones out of the closet, brought back memories I needed to refresh myself with, and reminded myself of some valuable lessons.

As the father of ten children, I am often called on for advice, and I always try to make my kids understand that any advice I offer is a gift. Just as with any other gift, once you give it, it's no longer yours. It belongs to those you've given it to, and it's theirs to do with as they see fit. That's the spirit in which I hope you read what I have to say.

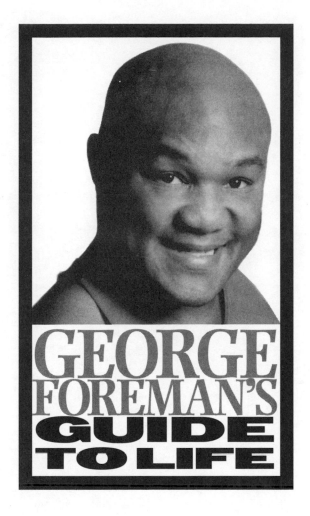

GEORGE FOREMAN'S GUIDE TO LIFE

heart you know it's not right for you. Your friends can tell you it's bad for you, that you've got to get out of it. But you're not going to make a move until you're ready. It's the same whether you're telling yourself to leave or someone else is telling you.

Wisdom is nothing more than a covenant with the truth. I made a pledge to myself long ago that no matter how much the truth hurts, I would accept it and hold myself to it. That is all wisdom is. To be able to see a lie or an injustice, you have to first look inside yourself, searching every corner of your mind, looking to clean every bit of your conscience. If you do this from day to day, the gift is complete: You can take advice from yourself.

Even if you have never found yourself without someone to turn to, your parents or your spouse or your best friend might not always be there, just as I won't always be there for my daughter. One day, you will have dreams, hopes, and disappointments so personal that you will not be able to tell those folks or anyone else about them. These you have to figure out for yourself.

Another reason it's so important for you to be able to trust yourself is that long after anyone else gives you advice, they will have forgotten what they told you. You're the only one who will have to live with the decisions you made. There is one person who has to look out for you always with the greatest intentions. That person is you. You will no doubt meet many people in this life, as I have, people who

DON'T TAKE MY ADVICE

I GOT AN E-MAIL not long ago from one of ł grown daughters who lives far from home telling me hc lonely she sometimes is; and that there is no one in her l right now to look to for advice. I know how she feels; I' been in that same place. Because no matter how bless you are to have loving relationships with family and frien there are times in nearly everyone's life when you feel t same way, when you say to yourself, "Who should I turn tc

The answer is simple: you. The real answers you ¿ looking for are inside of you. The hard part is being able *hear* them. Listening to yourself is no different than bei able to listen to what someone else tells you. Say you're i relationship that you really want to work but deep in yc will love you, who will try to provide for you and instruct you along the way. But even if other people are there to love you, it's important to remember that, ultimately, they are just like you. They are human beings, with all their own fears, trying like everybody else to make it through each day. No one has all the answers; otherwise, why would people have so many fears?

Who you take advice from says a lot about who you are. I have been a few different people in my life, but I now have a person who I respect and trust: me. And until you reach that place in life you are at the mercy of fate.

BE YOURSELF

WHEN I WAS about twelve years old, my mom sent me to see my cousin James in prison. I still don't know what he was serving time for, but I've come to understand why she wanted me to go with his family to visit him: She tried anything that might keep me from ending up there myself.

Unfortunately, that's not the lesson I came away with that day. James came into the waiting room with hundreds of other men, each one wearing identical white pants and big shirts. As I sat and watched with James's younger brother, Willie, one man came through the door who I couldn't take my eyes off. He wasn't any bigger or taller than the others, but he stood out from the rest of the men like the sun from the clouds. Even though he was dressed the same, *his* uniform somehow seemed tailor-made. The prison seemed like his castle, and he, a king. It even seemed like the guards at the jail worked for him. Finally, when Willie and I got up our nerve to ask James who he was, he told us, "He's a slugger"—a boxing term I'd never heard before that means that person is a hard hitter.

I left the prison that day thinking I wanted to be just like that man. He had no luxurious clothes or fine shoes or money, but he seemed to be everything I wanted to be: He commanded attention. Back then, the people I admired were the street fighters others feared. My role models were troublemakers—guys who had either been to jail or were most likely on their way. I thought anyone with a big, long scar down his face was worthy of being my hero. I wanted so much to be tough I even wore a Band-Aid on *my* cheek.

From that point on, I tried to put the pieces together to cut as imposing a figure as the guy in prison. When I saw a John Wayne movie, I would try to copy his walk. I wanted sideburns, a mustache, and beard like Jimmy Brown's, and I tried everything to get hair to grow on my face. Later, after I became a boxer, I watched how the people I'd put on a pedestal behaved around others. Sonny Liston was a bully, and I thought that was how you ought to act when you became a big-timer. Once when I ran into Brown and Walt Frazier at a jazz club in Harlem and they brushed me off, I thought to myself, "So that's how stars should behave!" I filed those lessons away so I could make sure I did the same. Even after I became heavyweight champ, I never bought anything unless I saw that someone I admired had it first: a car like this movie star, a suit like that singer, side-burns and a haircut like someone else. I wanted to be like my heroes. But before I knew it, I had bypassed being like them; I had become them. I had become so many people.

Then one night in 1977, I lost a fight in Puerto Rico to Jimmy Young by unanimous decision. Afterward, in the dressing room, I was sure I was dying, and it was my life I was fighting for. I saw everything I had ever worked for—money, homes, cars, fame—crumble like ashes. That experience changed me. After that, all I wanted was my *life—my* life. But having spent all those precious years trying to be like so many other people, I didn't even know who I was.

About a year later, as I was trying to trim my hair with a set of clippers, I accidentally cut a big "S" into the top of my head. I tried everything I could to correct it, but nothing helped, so finally I shaved it all off. When I looked in the mirror, I was so ashamed I put on a ski hat so no one else could see how I really looked. I intended to wear it until my hair grew back. But one day I forgot to put the hat on, and by the time I realized it, people had already snickered at me. I was as embarrassed as if I'd walked out in public without clothes on. When I studied my bald reflection, though, I rec-ognized a person I hadn't seen since I was a boy. I saw *me.* Looking back was the face I was born with, the boy my mom had always loved. I said to myself, "You are healthy, you have a home and all the things you've ever dreamed of, and yet you're ashamed of yourself because you don't look

I named all my sons George Edward Foreman, not because I couldn't think of a better name, but to lay down a foundation for them in life. I'm holding George V, whom we call "Red," when he was about one week old. The photo was taken in 1991, shortly before I fought Evander Holyfield.

like other people." You can't hide from yourself; I tried that for too long. I decided to leave the hat at home for good.

That's when I realized why I had admired that man in prison all those years earlier: He was the only person there who liked himself; he was exactly who he wanted to be. He wore his clothes like he loved them. While all the other men tried to act tough, he only had to be himself. My cousin and I had seen this man from the inside out.

From that day on, I have stood in front of any mirror with pride—brushing my teeth, shaving, or sometimes simply to admire the man God has made of me. I feel completely at peace. My only true goal is to be the same guy tomorrow that I am today. Who I am has nothing to do with what I look like on the outside, only with what I feel on the inside. It has nothing to do with what I wear but with how I treat others. My identity doesn't come from my success but from the pride my wife and children have in me. I am me, and I like it. I am alive today with happiness for life itself.

I still admire others. I wish I could dance like Gregory Hines, shoot baskets like Michael Jordan, even act in movies like Robert De Niro. Still, I don't want to be anyone else but myself. I found out the best person I could be was George Foreman. Life is such a short journey. I tell my kids, "Spend it being yourself. Never carry anyone else along inside yourself." That makes it too hard. When you find yourself, hold on with all your might.

SELF-ESTEEM

THE FANCIEST GYMS I see these days have weights to tone every single muscle in your body and rows of heavy-duty machines like treadmills and rowing machines to shape up your heart. These are all good for your health, there's no doubt about it. But there's an extra piece of equipment you have to have to live a healthy life that you can't find inside a gym; you have to find it inside of *you*: self-esteem. Having pride in yourself is what protects you so that even when other people disapprove of who you are or what you look like or the job you do, you hold on to who you are and what you believe in. And you hold on tight. Having self-esteem means that you're not going to give up something that's important to you, whether it's your virginity or your independence or your ego, just because you think someone will like you better for

9

having changed. Believe me, if another person doesn't like you the way you are, there's not much you can do to change their mind.

If someone you're attracted to doesn't like the way your waist looks now, what are you going to do—alter your waist size? If they do like you because you went out and reshaped yourself, you're not much of anything anyway. You've got to reshape yourself to make someone love you? *You* love you. *You* fall in love with you. Look in the mirror and gaze up at who you are and appreciate that. Then, if you want, go out and find someone who appreciates you as much as you do. But don't say, "I'm going to go out and get a twenty-nine-inch waist *for her*, I'm going to buy a Mustang *for her*. I'm going to get a Cadillac *for him*." If someone doesn't like you when you're walking, they're hardly going to like you just because you've bought a nice car. And if they do start treating you differently because you got a car or you suddenly hit the jackpot, then you've got to have enough pride in yourself not to fall for their sudden attention. It's not about *you*, and it usually means they'll drop you just as quickly as they befriended you as soon as the next flashy person comes along.

I learned this lesson when I was a teenager. After I finished the Job Corps program in California, my coach Doc Broadus sent me a plane ticket back there so I could keep boxing, and he got me a job as a dishwasher in the kitchen to help me support myself. I was also the best floor mopper!

10

I used to help all the guys in the kitchen out with their jobs, and in return they would always give me extra food. Still, I didn't really have any friends. The only person who even treated me as a true equal was Doc Broadus. That's because most of the guys I lived with in the bachelor officer's quarters (we called it the BOQ).

Members of the 1968 United States Olympic boxing team. I'm the tall, serious-looking one in the back row. Ronnie Harris *(front row, left)*, the team leader, went on to win a gold medal and become a pro champion.

11

were teachers or highly educated counselors. The time I had spent as a corpsman made many of them uncomfortable, and they looked down on the fact that I worked in a kitchen instead of a classroom. It wasn't just my background, either. They had more money than I did, and most of them drove nice cars.

Each weekend, after I had been paid, I would hope to get a ride just a few miles off base and back so I could get a sandwich (pastrami and cheese was my favorite). Most of the guys in the BOQ knew I needed a lift; they'd see me waiting downstairs in the lobby. Instead of helping me out, though, the ones with cars would usually go back up to their rooms to wait me out. Sometimes, if I'd go back upstairs for just a moment, they would rush down, get in their cars, and drive away. Later, when they came back, they'd lie, saying, "I wish I'd known you needed a ride." It got to the point that I would just stay in my room on weekends so they could come and go without worrying that I would ask for a ride.

One night, after I had left the kitchen, I saw Mr. Tyree Lyons, the head chef, waiting for a friend at the BOQ. I stopped and chatted for a moment, then started to rush off to my room so the two of them could leave me without any embarrassment. But as I headed off, Tyree called out, "Where are you going tonight?" I said, "I'm going to watch a TV show." I was trying to be a little proud. He said, "Stay for a moment and then you can ride to Oakland with us."

After that, Tyree would come by once a week and take me somewhere to get a sandwich.

After I won the Olympic gold medal, the same guys who used to avoid me would see me in the TV room and ask, "George, you need a ride?" I would answer, "No, Tyree is coming by soon." This was my self-esteem talking. And its voice was loud and clear: If I was not good enough for the people who owned cars in the beginning, being famous should not suddenly make me acceptable. I was the same young man who had cleaned myself up and dressed well before I asked for a ride. If they didn't like me without the gold medal, they should know that I was no different with a medal. I made a decision that it was better to stay in my room and be with my best friend—me—until someone who really liked me and accepted me for who I was came by, like Tyree.

Later, when I went to Jamaica to fight Joe Frazier, I took Tyree with me. He was not only my cook, he was a true friend. He liked me just the same whether I was scrubbing pots in a mess hall or winning the title fight. Just being myself had always been a good enough credential for him.

THERE'S ALWAYS A REASON TO SMILE

I TRY never to let my children see me sad. When my mother died a few years ago, they asked me, "Dad, how did you manage not to cry when you preached at her funeral?" I did cry; just not in front of them.

I'm not saying you shouldn't ever feel sad. But I believe children, especially when they're young, need to feel they can depend on their parents. They need consistency. And when they see their mom or dad upset, they get worried and scared.

There's also another reason to put the best face on things. My mother and my aunts passed on to me the firm belief that life is never so bad you can't find something to smile about. Even if they were just out of the hospital, all stitched up, they didn't focus on their pain. Instead, they would turn their attention to their visitors. It was always, "How are *you*, baby?" to anyone who came by.

There's probably not an adult in this world who hasn't been through some difficulty—they've been divorced or lost someone they loved, or maybe they've been seriously sick themselves. But you can't let your troubles and sorrow define who you are or how you treat other people.

A while back, I met a man in California who had a series of numbers tattooed on his arm. When I asked him what it was, someone whispered to me, "He was in a German concentration camp." "But," I said to my children, "his was the brightest smile of all the people I met that day."

When I went back to boxing at age thirty-seven, things were so serious: It seemed as if Mike Tyson wanted to kill everybody, and athletes weren't accessible. The rare times they were, it was always without a smile. They were so untouchable. But I knew the reporters by name and would laugh at their old stories (I was around when so many took place). The press wrote about my fighting a tomato can. Others would have been angry, but I would see them and laugh with them about it. Or they'd say, "George, people are saying you are fighting guys from the dead. What do you have to say?" "Well," I'd answer, "they are only saying it because it's true." They loved the fact that somebody was having fun.

I've told my kids there were many boxers who were better than I was, but there was no one happier. Every time I was in front of a camera, I'd smile. I would never let it catch me looking sad. I understood that the people watching had their own set of problems; they didn't need to hear about mine before they ate or slept or went to work. I saw it as my job to make them feel good. I would never get serious on TV. (The time to get serious was in the ring.) Every answer would end with a joke. Even if they couldn't hear me, they could see me smiling. And those who couldn't see me could still hear me, and start to smile themselves. People would invite me into their homes, so to speak, because I would never get too serious on them; I was safe.

Interviews were hard to get in those days. After you would beg for a spot on a local sports show, they would give you only a few seconds. I would wait for the spotlights, attack with a smile, and then tell the sportscaster about my age, my weight, and my new belly-bump punch. This would have folks calling and asking questions of the networks. I had gone ten years without watching TV, and I saw when I put it back on that it was always the funny stuff that would make me stop flipping the remote. I decided to meet everybody with a smile, so I would never have to put on an act. I was going to be the happiest man alive on TV. I heard a man say, "You can't beat happy." Well, I was Old Happy.

Sammy Davis, Jr., was a close friend who taught me, "You gotta make them love you," one of the most valuable lessons of my life. This picture was taken in 1976 at Caesars Palace in Las Vegas.

Even today I keep my kids in tune with this philosophy. I tell them, "Keep your smile; it will be your health. There will be better students in college; but you can be the happiest about being there. Don't let anyone beat you at this. Have it said when someone meets you: 'I met the nicest person in the world,' because you have a smile, joke, or time for the least of them."

I have tried to teach my kids not only *to* smile but explain why they *should*. I say, "When you have some extra money and you are happy, I never see you running around telling everyone; you keep it to yourself. When you have hard knocks, you should be able to conceal them as well. At evening's passing you will have your stroke of dawn." I want them to know that the world is not against them, no matter how bad things might sometimes seem. They say, "Daddy, you think the world is such a great place. You're always laughing." I say, "That's right." You have to smile while smiling times are here.

LIFE IS SHORT

A LOT OF PEOPLE try to eat right and exercise so they'll live a long time. Of course it's important to be as healthy as possible. Ultimately, though, we have no control over how long we're in this world. And even if we lived to be 969 years old, like old Methuselah, this life would still seem too short. That's why it's so important to recognize that *how* we live is at least as important as *how long* we live.

Too many people go out of this life counting the money they've accumulated instead of the amount of love they've given others. They're no more generous with their care and concern than they are with their wealth. They go to their grave saying things like, "I love you and I'd do anything for you, but just don't ask me to love your mother. I'm not going to help her out. She gets on my nerves, big time." In fact, some people are so stingy they die with a heap of possessions and no feelings of tenderness toward others at all.

People seem to completely forget that you bring nothing into this world and you won't take anything out, either— nothing, that is, but the love and respect you've earned throughout your life and the memories of what you've done for others. You can take what you stood for in life, that your children meant something to you, that your mother and father and friends meant something to you. You can't take anything else. It's fun to buy a few nice things, but understand that none of that leaves when you do. And there are certain things that are not for sale, anyway. You can't buy your way into being a better person; it's something you earn every day.

My mother used to drink water out of leftover jelly and fruit jars. She could have afforded a set of fine crystal glassware if she'd wanted (or I would have bought them for her!), but she didn't care about that. She lived a simple life until the day she died.

The point is that whether she saved those jars instead of throwing them away or paid a lot of money for hand-blown glasses at some fancy shop, it didn't make any difference in the long run. None of her drinking glasses went with her. What she did take was the knowledge of how much we cared for her. And the most valuable thing she could possibly have left my sisters and me is the memory of how fine a person she was. What she left us is the knowledge that she loved us and watched over us and prayed for us and kept us close.

Foreman women *(left to right)*: My sister Mary, the fourth of my mom's seven children; my mom, Nancy Ree Foreman; and my oldest sister, Willie Mae. The photo was taken when my mom was ninety-four.

I have a picture in my mind of her standing over a gas heater. We didn't have any electricity when I was growing up— not even a real stove to cook on. So my mom would get up early in the morning and put on a pot of beans with some fat meat on top of the heater. It took so long to cook, she'd just let it sit there all day.

21

Then she'd just drop some meal in there and mix it up; she wouldn't even try to fry any cornbread. I'd be sitting there watching and thinking, "I'm going to beat up all my sisters if they try to get some of those soft, tender beans." I'd fight them for that. Whenever I miss her, I'm always reminded of that pan of food. That was love to me; she gave us whatever she had. And I've never been able to find anyone who can make that stuff taste the same as my mother did.

The love and the memories my mother left us are the best anyone could hope for. When you get ready to leave this life, all you're going to take with you are your deeds. How much did you love other people? Did you love all your kids the same? Did you love everyone else's kids? As for the fine china, the diamond rings, the nice cars, and the gorgeous handmade suits—they all stay behind.

Most of us have lived long enough to see the high and mighty, the rich and famous, pass out of this life. So we know they leave just like everyone else: There's a final second and that's it. Nothing else is taken. It's a strong lesson about how fruitless it is to strive for the things you'll lose anyway. Strive to gain things you can take with you—those are the things that matter.

BAD HABITS

WHEN I WAS a teenager, I had a lot of habits I'm not proud of today. I ran around drinking cheap wine. I was addicted to cigarettes. Many days, when I was on my last dime, I would even choose a pack of cigarettes over a sandwich.

I also chose cigarettes over football. Our junior-high coach—we called him "Bear" after the University of Alabama coach, Paul "Bear" Bryant—was a strict man whom we respected and feared in equal measure. I was especially afraid of him because of his unforgiving views on smoking. He constantly lectured about its adverse effects on athletes. And when he caught any of his players with a cigarette, his preferred form of punishment was a wooden paddle applied with an unsparing hand. After he spotted me smoking one day, rather than face his disappointment in me, I dropped out of football. And since my love of the game was the

23

only thing still keeping me in school, I dropped out of that, too.

My habit started with stealing cigarettes from my parents. I would cough and get crazy on purpose to make my friends laugh. But after I tried to quit, I found that something I had begun as a joke wasn't funny at all. I'd say, "I'm through," and within an hour, I'd be back smoking again. Or I'd throw a new pack out of the window; then, at night, I'd go outside looking for it. If the cigarettes had gotten wet, I'd put them on something warm to dry them out. When I went looking for a job and I'd see a half-smoked butt in an office building, I would stay behind, sneak the butt into my pocket, straighten it out, and then ask a person for a light—as if I had let my cigarette go out by mistake.

Even when I started boxing, I kept on smoking for a while. I'd hear athletes say that smoking shortens your breath; that you can't be good at anything if you smoke. I was so ashamed to ask for a cigarette by that time, I'd collect pieces of tobacco and roll them in brown paper from a grocery bag. The fire would shoot up and sometimes singe my eyebrows.

Cigarettes had me. I could not stop!

All that changed one day while I was working at a gym in California. I got a letter from my oldest sister. She told me that one of our other sisters, who was pregnant, was in desperate financial shape—sometimes she and her other kids went hungry, and Willie Mae was writing to ask me to help out. When I sent her my whole paycheck, she wrote me back saying how proud she was of me and how much I had helped the children. It was so nice, she said, to have a brother that had made something of himself and who still loved his family. She had never called me "brother" before. "I am going to pray for you," she said. The idea that my family needed me made me feel so good about myself that I never again could sneak a butt from an ashtray or roll smokes like a thief in the dark.

For me, quitting finally had nothing to do with will-power, or even with the fact that smoking prevented me from being the best boxer I could be. I stopped because I chose the love and care of my family over my weakness. I would still wake up wanting a smoke as badly as I had before, but the love of my family exerted an even stronger pull over me.

I tried so hard to quit, I know what a battle it is to do so. That's why I tell youngsters these days, "If you start smoking, you do it for yourself. But if you never start, it's a decision you make for your family—especially for the little brother who imitates every move you make."

THINK BEFORE YOU SPEAK

I HAVE a friend who had been put in charge of a large, well-known company. He has always been a nice man (and I believe he still is), so I was especially surprised to hear one of the foulest cusswords come out of his mouth. At the time, he was dressed in a suit, sitting at the head of a conference table running an important meeting. In all the years I had known him, his mouth had always been pretty clean. Maybe he had sworn here and there. This time, he let that ugly word rip almost as if to say, "I am the boss; I answer to no one." Of course if he were just any other man or woman working at that firm, people would have warned him to watch his tongue. But since he calls the shots, everybody just kept quiet and dropped their heads so they didn't have to look him in the eye.

I am no stranger to swearing. As a boy, I couldn't wait to get a handle on a few choice words you would never find in a family dictionary. I made it a point to hang around places where I'd run into a crowd of rough-around-the-edges grown-ups just to broaden my vocabulary. Pretty soon, I could let go with some of the crudest words ever invented. Later, when I was a young man and met the great boxer Sonny Liston, one of the things that really impressed me about him was that he managed to use cusswords I'd never heard. He'd say, "This dirty this," and, "This dirty that." It wasn't long before I took up his bad language, adding it to my own. When I met up with other fighters, I would choose how I said things to be as vulgar as possible because I wanted them to go tell others, "George said so and so." I tried to use language as a way to make people fear me. It was the same with everyone: Cussing, it seems, was the international language of boxing. Whenever I ran into men who wanted to impress me with their strength, they would always greet me with, "Hello you Bad———." This was to let me know, "You might be a force to reckon with, but I am no pushover." I knew it was all swagger; that my hands were a lot tougher than their words.

It wasn't until after I started raising children and running into old friends who greeted me the same as always that I realized that words *can* hurt. They can be just as powerful and destructive as any weapon: They can escalate a situation so the next thing that happens is that people start pushing each other around or they bring out a real weapon. I became ashamed for my friends and protective of my kids. I told my children that people who use bad language are just trying to push their weight around; that they're stuck in childhood, still trying to prove themselves. I taught them to keep away— just like you teach your kids to keep their distance from a hot stove. And so they have always walked away from adults who talked like that with a shake of their heads and a laugh. But I hear so many guys and girls light it up with bad language, with no respect for anyone else. These kids have no idea that what they say and how they say it doesn't prove their strength, it proves their weakness—and their ignorance. Like me when I was a kid, they hear what adults say and copy them because they think it means *they're* grown up, too.

The more I've traveled around in the world, the more I realize how important it is to find the right words to express yourself. It means the difference between communicating and putting people off. Just as important, you never know who you're going to offend with bad language. Watching how you say things is a measure of respect. These days, you'll be at a dinner party and most people will ask, "Do you mind?" before they pull out a cigarette. But no one ever asks, "Mind if I swear?" Even if cursing doesn't have the same long-term health effects as secondhand smoke, in some

I am standing with my hero, Joe Louis, in 1976. Whenever he spoke, I would stop everything and give him my ear.

ways it's not so different: You could be hurting others and not even be aware of the damage you're causing.

You can't ask to be seated in a swearing or a nonswearing section at a restaurant, but you shouldn't need a law to remind you to always be sensitive to other people's feelings anyway. All you have to do is stop to consider that some people might not want to be subjected to certain words, even if you feel they're okay. It's about thinking before you speak.

WHAT GOES AROUND COMES AROUND

WHEN I was a boy growing up in Houston, my friends and I used to mug people just because we could. The streets in my neighborhood, the Fifth Ward, were so mean, the area was nicknamed "the Bloody Fifth." I was no better than any other kid there. I dropped out of junior high school. I smoked cigarettes and drank cheap wine. I relied on my fists to make my way in life. After I spent two years in the Job Corps—first in Oregon and then in California—I came back to Houston, and I was a pretty good boy on the right road. What I had learned in the Job Corps helped me pass my GED. I had never felt so proud.

Before long, though, I got my old wine in me and I started back down the same dangerous path I'd been on before. One night at a party I got so drunk, I beat up a couple of guys over a girl. The next day, my swollen fist wasn't the only sign of what I'd done. There was also a warrant at my mother's house for my arrest. The guys had pressed assault charges. I didn't even know what a warrant was, I just knew the police were looking for me and that I was in big trouble.

I went down to the police station like the warrant ordered. When the desk sergeant read it, he said, "You know, I could lock you up right now." But then he gave me a choice: Pay a one-hundred-dollar fine or go to jail. I took off out of there as fast as I could. When I got home, I told my mother what had happened. I believed I probably hadn't escaped jail for long; we didn't have that kind of money. I didn't know what to do.

Fortunately, my mother did. She had a longtime friend, Mr. Thomas, who was old and sick and had no family to take care of him. He rented a room about a mile from where Mom lived. She worried about him, and from time to time, she sent me down there with a home-cooked meal. I was glad to take it to him; as mismatched as we were in age and experience, we struck up a kind of friendship. When I took him a plate, I would sit for a few minutes and he would tell me stories about his past. He liked that, and, in my own way, I did, too. He was about the only person I knew who didn't seem to care that I was not a model citizen. To him, I was.

When I got into trouble with the police, my mom went to Mr. Thomas and told him what had happened. He loaned her the money and she went right downtown and paid off the fine. While everyone else saw me as a bad boy, Mr. Thomas saw the good in me. He was willing to believe that my behavior was a mistake and that I would learn from the experience. That's what saved me from jail.

Soon after that, my old friend and boxing coach in the Job Corps, Doc Broadus, another person in my life who somehow managed to see my potential, cashed in his paycheck and sent me a one-way plane ticket back to California. That's when my boxing career began in earnest. And when I figured out how belligerent drinking made me, I gave it up altogether.

> A parade was given in my honor at the Job Corps Center in Pleasanton, California, after I won the Olympic gold medal in 1968. Walking with me *(to my left)* is Doc Broadus. He is saying what he had said all along: "I told you so."

Not everyone always showed the same kind of faith in me, however. I make sure to tell all my children about the girl I dated soon after I began my pro boxing career. She was from the same down-and-out neighborhood I was. Back then, I could never figure out how I'd managed to

miss her growing up. She was someone special—pretty
through and through—and after we dated for about a year,
we thought about getting married. It was her mom who
put a quick end to those plans. She told me, "I have put my
life into my daughter so she could get a good education and
be something, not just somebody's girlfriend." She told me
to find another girl to mess with. I knew I wasn't really
ready to settle down, anyway.

I stayed away after that and went on with my life as best

I could, dogged by one bad relationship after another. Finally, years later, I tried to put things right between us. By that time, I understood too well why I had never seen her in the Fifth Ward when we were teenagers: Her mom had kept her away from fellows like me—guys who were up to no good, who were always messing up. She'd saved up her money to send her daughter to college so that she could dream big. I called her and said, "There was nothing wrong with you; I was just not a good person."

I tell my kids that story because I want them to understand that you can't erase the bad you've done, you have to take responsibility for your actions, acknowledge and apologize for your behavior, and do what you can to try and set things right. But I also try to make sure they know that there is no such thing as a bad person in this world; that you can always change the way you behave.

Here's a case to prove it. A few years ago, I was getting ready to do a commercial for Oscar Mayer. I never stopped to wonder why they'd hired me; I was just grateful to be making some money. But before the filming got under way, the people shooting it asked to have a talk with me. They said, "George, while we were writing this, we asked around about who would be a good person to feature in the spot. Someone spoke up and said, 'Have you seen all the work George Foreman is doing in Houston with the kids, how he took his own money and started a youth center? Let's give this to him.'"

The point is not that the universe always rewards good with good and repays bad with bad. Everyone knows a person who brings nothing but joy to others and she still gets sick or someone who's the perfect dad and he still loses his job. What I'm saying is that people are usually drawn to those who do good. They want to be associated with them; and sometimes, like Mr. Thomas, they're willing to go the extra mile to help them out. By the same token, if someone has been dishonest or hurtful, others usually want to run the other way.

That's why I tell my kids, "Keep being good, and good will always come to you."

DON'T BE AFRAID TO CHANGE

NOT THAT long ago, one of my sons called me up to talk about a new job he'd been offered. "What should I do?" he wanted to know. It all sounded pretty good to me. The pay was better, and it came with some nice fringe benefits. But when I called him back a couple of days later, he sounded as though he had made up his mind to turn it down. "They only give year-to-year contracts," he said. "The guy I work for now has been so good to me. And you know they probably just want me for my name, anyway."

That's when I paid him a visit. I knew these weren't the things that were really keeping him from taking the job; they were just convenient excuses to stay put. Sure enough, when I took a good look at him, I recognized exactly what I had seen so many times in myself: fear of change. Change of any kind scares most people so much that they don't even get as far as my son got: They don't allow for something new to become a possibility before their anxiety talks them out of it. They never get that job offer or make an offer on a new house; they've already come up with a dozen reasons why whatever it is won't work. Some people can even be in a horrible situation, and they still feel more comfortable sticking with what they know. The known makes them feel safe, even if they know how bad it is. *Who* they are seems tied to *where* they are and *what* they're doing.

I have struggled with the same thing. In the late 1980s, after ten years out of boxing, I was content being a family man at home with my kids; I'd meet with teachers after school and drive to the supermarket in my little six-cylinder car. I knew that if I went back into the ring that would all change. As much as I wanted to regain my heavyweight title and to make money to fund my youth center, I also liked things just the way they were. I asked myself, "Aren't you just going to mess up a good thing?"

Often, the people you're the closest to have an investment in keeping everything the way it's always been. Because people are like dominoes: When one person makes a move, everyone around them has to make adjustments, too. When I was making my decision about reentering boxing, we were walking to the car after a movie one night and one of my daughters said to me, "Dad, you see we can come to the movies now and no one bothers us. If you go back to boxing, it will mean the end of all this. Everywhere you go, they'll call your name and ask for an autograph." That was her fear talking. Even my wife told me, "You are going to get killed," to frighten me away from returning to boxing. Later, she admitted she was more afraid of the ways I might change—and the way those changes might affect the whole family—than of my getting hurt. Would I go back to wearing those fancy clothes and hanging out with that old fast crowd?

When I went to see my child, I told him about the day not too long ago that I went to the offices of Salton, the appliance maker, and the president made an offer to buy my part of the George Foreman grill. Even though the money was more than I could ever have dreamed of, I was afraid. I said to myself, "This is my job; this is what I do now. If I sell it, what will I do with my life? Where will I belong?"

So many of us think if we change jobs, addresses, schools, even hairdos, that we have to change who we are. But who we are is like an oak; we are planted so much deeper than we think. And we usually have the answers of what to do inside us—with all our fears—all along.

I've learned that you shouldn't be afraid to change; instead, be afraid to stay where you are in life. Stepping out sometimes is what makes you good, better, and even the best at what you're doing. If you let fear of change rule you, you will live never knowing there is a fuller life out there that is yours for the taking.

The scales are beginning to look good again. After starting out weighing 315 when I made my comeback in the late 1980s, I am down to a fighting 245, ready to reach for the title again. By this time (around 1990), the people who had laughed at my initial efforts were now pulling for me.

HOTEL

SCALES

the referee
is not that
d that they
usually no
one to pull

was blind-
wife of six
ter had to
a, my ac-
gs behind

FOOTBALL PLAYERS expect
to give them a penalty for piling on. But real life
fair: When difficulties pile up—and I've noticed
seldom seem to occur just one at a time—there's
one to throw down a flag. *You* have to be the c
yourself out from under life's burdens.

During one short period several years ago, I
sided by one painful event after another: My
months told me she was leaving, my little daugh
move back to live with her mom in Minneso
countant confessed he'd invested my life's savir

40

my back in deals that had gone bust. What's more, when he came to deliver the news, he brought a friend whom he probably considered a bodyguard with him in case I threatened to hurt him. I had lost not only all my money but, even more than that, some people in my life whom I loved and trusted. I didn't think I could cope with all that heartache and loss.

What brought me back to myself was that as a preacher, I had pledged to make my life an example in both good times and bad. I told myself that even though my accountant did me wrong, he would have to answer to himself—·not to me. I understood that if I had given him the impression he needed protection from me physically, I was the one who had a lot of work to do. After that, I was no longer concerned about getting my money back or getting even. I just wanted to act in such a way that the tough-looking guy who came to protect my accountant would say to himself, "He doesn't need me; he's not in physical danger." That was the person I was striving to be. And once I got my grounding, evil passed me by.

When times are tough, you don't have to be a preacher to answer the question, "Who do you want to be?" I constantly remind every one of my kids, "Remember that evil lurks where disappointment lodges." Make sure you don't let hard times shape you into another person—one you wouldn't be proud of.

When I was a boxer in the 1970s, I was hit in the face by

Joe Frazier, knocked out by Muhammad Ali, and knocked down a couple of times by Ron Lyle before I got up and won. All of the fights had one thing in common: When they were over, I could hardly remember the pain. I forgot my weak knees, the cuts, the blood in my eyes. If not for films of the fights, I would have put them totally out of my mind. It's the same when you hit rough times: Don't let the disappointment and pain lodge inside.

With life there is pain and still more pain, but even with it all, there is always a reason to smile: a beat of music to make you lift your feet and dance; a piece of chocolate to sweeten up a moment. With death, as far as we know, there is no pain, only silence.

I was taking a lonely jog in 1976, on a dirt road in Marshall, Texas. It was one of my last runs before I left boxing the first time in 1977 to become a preacher.

YOU'RE NEVER TOO OLD TO FIGHT

THE DAY I turned thirty-seven, I broke down and cried. I just did not want to be that age; it seemed like a death sentence. The people I knew who were that age didn't use words like "promise" and "potential" to talk about themselves and their futures; they said things like, "I feel stuck," or, "I'm just an old has-been." I thought that's what another birthday meant for me, too. So I cried off and on the whole day. Then, I asked myself, "Now what am I going to do with my life?"

While I was trying to figure it out, I spent a day driving

around the Fifth Ward in Houston, where I grew up. I visited every house we had lived in, and we moved a lot when I was a kid. My mom brought home about twenty-six dollars a week, and when it came down to a choice between groceries and rent—which it often did—the rent lost out. So we'd pack up and go on to the next place. Sometimes we would move away, and then, a year later, we'd rent the same house again. But all the places we lived had a few things in common: They were small, dark, and infested with rats. Someone told my sisters and me stories at Christmas of a big man who would come down the chimney and leave gifts for little children. I used to wonder where we were supposed to leave this guy some food when we were always in a house without even a stove to cook on—not to mention a chimney.

One house in particular broke my heart. It reminded me of the day my mom sent me to a little corner store right across the street from our house. I didn't have anything to wear to school, and so I had to stay home. Mom had given me a note for the lady who owned the store. I couldn't read yet, so Mom said to me, "Take this letter to the store and give it to the lady, and wait for her answer." The store owner handed me back the note, and told me to tell my mom, "We don't have any." So I went home with that message. "You mean she didn't have any collard greens," my mom asked. I said, "Oh yes she did. I saw them right in front of the counter." How I wished at that moment that I could read and have spared my mom some heartache and embarrassment. She started to cry, and she told me, "All I asked her was to let me have two bunches of greens to feed my children and that I would give her twenty-five cents at the end of the week."

I just sat there in my car with every memory of the past coming back. I remember not knowing how to write the figure "3" and how much I wished I could learn before I went back to school the next day. I thought about how all I had ever wanted to do was to learn how to hit the speed bag and skip rope like the boxers I had seen on TV. I kept saying to myself, "I can never learn how to do this." I had heard of men running a whole mile nonstop. But at six-teen, I couldn't even run a whole lap—a quarter-mile— around the track. How could I think of ever being a boxer or of going to the Olympics when my body didn't even have true muscles? All the guys at the gym would take off their shirts to play basketball, but not me. It hurt me for anyone to see my body. But the day I fought Joe Frazier when I was twenty-four, I took off my shirt and people said, "Look at that body; it is the perfect boxing body." Where once I could not write "3," now I could say the alphabet backward: zyxwvutsrqponmlkjihgfedcba.

When I was young, I started with nothing and I was able to build a dream. By the time I was thirty-seven, my mom had her own house with all the good food she could ever ask for. Her house had not only a fine stove but TVs, spare bedrooms, and two cars in the driveway. At thirty-seven years of age, I was able to run ten miles just for fun. I could hit the speed bag with my eyes closed. I could skip rope in my sleep. I had a home for all my kids, chimneys everywhere, an abundance of food. Not only that, but I was mentally and emotionally stronger than I'd ever been before. I knew what I was made of. Maybe we didn't get those greens when I was a little boy, but I grew up to become the heavyweight champion of the world. I had made something of my life at a time when I had no hope. If I could go ten rounds in the past fearing that I wasn't ready, just think what I could do with my experience now.

Of course that's not what the promoters and sportswriters said when I announced in 1987 that I was making a comeback after ten years of retirement. "He's too old," they said. "He's too fat. Someone will hurt him." But then I would drive back to my old neighborhoods and ask myself what *I* thought. The answer was that I had more inner resources than I'd ever had before. I had read books about other men and women who had been told they would fail because of their age. I understood that some of those people had given up simply because they believed what others said about them.

When I got back into boxing, I didn't have the same body I had had ten years earlier or even the same speed, but I said to myself, "Get another style." I had to fight smarter. I had to concentrate on finding the shortcomings of the younger guys who were my opponents. I prayed not to be younger but to be the best I could be at my age.

I often tell my story to people who are about to lose their job after twenty years. "Start over," I say. I want people to believe that if I could go back and do the physical, mental, and emotional work it took to rebuild my boxing career then surely they can go back to college. I tell them, "If your company lays you off, it is their loss. Build another career. Remember when things were really hopeless, and you made it? Now you only have to repeat what you have already done."

Old age is not something that just happens to you, it's a choice you make. I wasn't going to allow anyone else to make the decision for me about how I would live the rest of my life. As long as you believe in yourself, you can still be productive. You can look in the mirror and cry as I did and give up as I started to do. Or you can look in that mirror at any age, and dream another dream. If it can be dreamed, it can be done!

THE USABLE PAST

PEOPLE ASK me all the time if I ever get tired of hearing about my fight with Muhammad Ali. What I usually tell them is that the fight—and losing to him—is a big part of my past. While it was one of the most painful experiences for me, if you were to take Ali and that eighth-round knockout he dealt me on that long-ago night in Africa out of my past, then there's a lot of my story that is no longer there.

It's important to claim your past—to know where you came from and how you have arrived where you are. But at the same time—and this is big—never forget that the past is what it is: gone on! That's why I have never been one to talk much about "the good old days." I don't want to interrupt other people's lives by being an ex-hero. I've always believed that nostalgia comes from people who want to think that yesterday was somehow better than today. You can sit around talking about how good life used to be and then you don't have any time left over to try to make today better. So that's one thing I've tried to refrain from. I try to let the past stay where it is and let today speak for itself.

Nonetheless, you don't want to just cut out pieces of your past. Making mistakes comes with living in this world, and all of us can learn from our mistakes. There have been many times when I wish I hadn't forgotten about some of the things I've *already* been through, some of the lessons I've learned, because, believe me, I could have saved myself a lot of trouble. You don't want to live life in a circle, always having to relearn the same things. You don't get very far that way.

Learn from your mistakes but don't be chained to them. The same is true for your background or your heritage. Never forget that you can be who you choose to be. So many kids are afraid they'll end up just like their parents. It can take work to pull off all those old layers, but you don't ever have to accept any version of yourself that does not fit who you want to become. I hear people say all the time, "Well, that's the way she grew up," or, "He is just like his dad." Well, that may be where you came from, but that's not where you have to stay. That doesn't have to be the direction you're heading. That may be who your father is, but

I showed Cassius Clay, Sr., what his son Muhammad Ali had done to my eye the day after I lost the 1974 "Rumble in the Jungle" and my heavyweight title to Ali.

that doesn't mean that's who you are. Nothing is in your blood if *you* don't want it to be. The buck stops with you!

I used to worry about this because my biological father was not the guy with his family that I wanted to be with mine. But I finally realized that the fact that he was absent from my life doesn't mean that I am absent in my own children's lives.

As for those people who ask if I ever get tired of hearing about Ali, I will always have a special place in my heart for him. He was a good boxer, and he is a better man.

FEELING YOUR PAIN

PEOPLE WHO give in to their pain are almost always destined to come in second or third in life. It's like runners in a race: One guy's knee starts hurting and he slows down to protect it; another guy's knee starts hurting, and all he can see ahead of him is the finish line. It's the people who stop to consider their hurt and heartache who usually fall short of their goals. Some even drop out altogether just because they experience a little disappointment or sorrow. You've got to play through your pain if you want to make it where you're going.

People on the sidelines rarely feel any pain. For the last few years, my wife and I have had season tickets for the men's pro basketball team in Houston. We look down and watch the

guys play, and if we get tired, we can sit back on a comfortable sofa and follow the game on a screen. There's even a place to put a wheelchair.

But it's a whole different story for the basketball players. Looking down from my seat, I can see them limping off the court, putting ice on their knees, lying on their backs, even going back to the dressing room to get medical treatment like stitches—whatever it takes for them to stay in the game.

The point is there is pain while you're playing; there is pain while you're in the game. Pain means you're in it. If you aren't feeling any twinges or pangs, it means you're out of it. You can't quit just because something hurts; you can't stop to feel sorry for yourself.

After I lost to Ali in October 1974, I didn't try to hide my swollen eye with dark glasses. The loss was tough for me, but this was my first lesson in reclaiming my past.

Not many people I've asked have ever heard of Buster Mathis. But if I ask those same folks if they've heard the name Joe Frazier, everybody's hand pops up. Buster Mathis was a boxer who was trying to get to the Olympics in 1964. He won all of the qualifying events. He even whipped Frazier. But then Buster hurt his hand and Frazier went to the Olympics instead. Buster Mathis could have won it all, but he gave in to his pain.

Here's a man who beat Smokin' Joe Frazier and no one's ever heard of him. That's why the one thing you've got to do is move past your pain. If you break your right hand, you have to start doing things with your left. If you break your left hand, start doing more things with your right. Believe me, there is no comfort in saying, "I almost made it."

Life is the same way. There is always a broken dream or a broken promise; there is always a broken heart. But if someone breaks your heart, you have to move past that empty feeling. If someone steals your money, you have to get over your anger and sense of vulnerability. Why? Because you have to get where you're going. People can take away everything else, but no one can take away your desire to get where you're going.

People break bones all the time. There have always been people who have had no choice but to work—people with families, people with responsibilities. If they broke their finger, they had to find a stick and wrap some tape around their finger. They had to deal with it and move on. Why? Because they had to get to where they were going. If you asked them why they didn't go to a doctor, they'd say, "I wouldn't have gotten my crop in. I've got all my stuff in the barn now."

If you want to live this good life, you have to understand that a little suffering and disappointment are bound to come with it. It's part of the package. If you're tired of all life's troubles, you don't get to say to yourself, "I think I'll hang around in the morgue for a day or two." The real residents of the morgue feel no pain. You could turn the temperature down to freezing in there and they wouldn't complain. You could hold a lit match to their finger and they wouldn't feel it burn.

In life, there's always going to be something to wake you up and let you know you're alive. You don't fall down and stay down; you don't give up just because you run into a little pain. You keep on fighting. After people leave this life, the electricity bill comes to their house. It might be six hundred dollars. But the people who died don't give it a second thought. Have you ever heard them complain? "Oh my God, these bills are killing me." It's different when you're alive. You can always tell when someone is living in a house because they start screaming about those bills. You can hear the mother or father telling the kids, "Close those windows, shut those doors, turn down the heat." The dead do not complain about bills. That's a job for the living.

After I had been boxing for a long time, I looked up one day and it was as though my hand had dried up. I tried to grip a little weight and I couldn't get my fingers around it. I could barely make a fist. So I went to a doctor and he stuck some needles in there. He said, "Can you feel this?" I said, "No." "How about this?" I said, "No." He said, "You've just about lost everything out of this arm." When I was boxing, I kept blocking shots with my hand and it apparently destroyed a nerve.

The first thought that came to mind was how I was going to conceal that from the doctors who would examine me for my boxing matches. I wasn't thinking, "What's wrong with my hand?" I didn't care; I had another hand. My fingers were closed together, and I thought, "How can

I conceal this from people who will say, 'Poor old George'?" I became an expert at concealing my hand. If someone was considering me for a commercial, they weren't going to see this right hand. I hid it. That's because my goal was to do something with my life. If anyone was ever asked if they'd heard of George Foreman, I wanted them to know my name. I didn't want to end up like old Buster.

Buster Mathis must not have realized that a broken heart hurts more than a broken hand. If you've ever watched the Winter Olympics, you've seen those young girls ice-skating. They always seem to be smiling. They suffer just as many aches and pains in practice as any hockey player with black shoe polish under his eyes. But they are afraid to tell their parents or coaches. They're afraid someone might say, "Next year, dear."

NEVER GIVE UP

YOU CAN'T wait for other people to decide that you're ready to do something if you want to get anywhere in this life. You've just got to step out there and do it. You have to tell yourself, "Maybe I'm not the best, but I'm going to persevere." If you can make the decision to stick with whatever you're doing, you can do anything you want. I know that probably sounds too simple to be true. There is always someone trying to get to the same goal you are, only they decide to stop halfway down the road. They say, "Who was I kidding? I don't want it." And when they walk away, they leave that road paved for you. All you've got to do is just keep moving ahead.

Determination counts for a lot. People who give up have a voice in their head that tells them, "That's enough. You can't do it. Maybe next time." There's always a reason to say, "Forget it." Accomplishing what you want usually takes a lot of hard work. There's the young guy or girl who wants to be a basketball player. Every afternoon while their friends are out laughing and cutting up, they're standing at a free-throw line shooting baskets over and over again. Or there's the computer whiz who wants to design new software and spends hours at the computer clicking away, trying to figure it out. It doesn't matter who you are or what stage of life you're in, if you ever submit to that voice that says, "This is too hard," you are not going anywhere. And quitting is contagious. If you stop one thing, you're going to stop another. You quit this, you're going to quit that. You run out on this, you're going to run out on the next thing, too.

Don't have that conversation with yourself where you say, "He's got more talent that I do," or, "She's faster than I am." Success depends on what's in your mind. I can tell you that being a boxing champion means more than physically waking up one morning and discovering a muscle or two. It happens from the tip of your toes all the way up to the crown of your head. Success is about your spirit.

Believe in yourself. It doesn't matter what people say about you. It matters what you say about yourself. I figure, don't let anyone tell you what you can't do. You just go out there and prove yourself. Don't let people talk you down. You let them all say, "He can't do it!" "She can't do it!" And then you let their voices fade away.

Believe me, there are enough naysayers around without

As a person who read my first whole books at age sixteen, the first time I wore a cap and gown was a proud day for my family and me. In 1999, I received an honorary degree as a Doctor of Law from Pepperdine University. Standing with me *(back row, left to right):* my daughter-in-law Anika (the wife of George, Jr.); my daughter Leola; my wife, Joan; George IV, and my sister-in-law Claudette. *(Front row):* George V. The baby is my granddaughter, Pamela. The child in front of me is Hillary, my brother's daughter.

my horse handling. The misstep was all my fault, just as we sometimes misread situations with other people. He was breeding and he didn't want me bothering with him then. He was saying, "Get out of my face."

Another time, I was going to break a horse—a mean little stallion. I got on his back and he bucked and finally I settled him down. He started to act like he was tame—he tricked me into believing that he was doing just fine. But I got on his back one day and he bucked me off. While I was falling, I could see him looking back try-

> I am holding the family dog, La'po, in training camp, about 1991, in Marshall, Texas, while getting in shape for my title comeback.

ing to measure, and he tried to kick my brains out. That horse aimed at my head. Fortunately, we're *both* still alive to this day. I couldn't very well be angry at a horse just for being a horse. I knew he was mean, and I let my guard down with him when I shouldn't have.

The point is I could forgive a horse for biting me, another for almost killing me. But it seems that people can rub us the wrong way and we're through with them overnight. We can forgive an animal and hold on to a grudge for years against another person.

When we do that, we've kind of sunk a little bit as far as human beings are concerned. Loving and caring for one another means constantly forgiving. If you've ever tried to housebreak a dog, you know it can take a long time. The dog

messes on the floor, and you say, "Well, it's just a puppy." Even when they get big and they make a mistake, you might say, "Well, I didn't let him out."

So if we can let an animal off for doing something that angers or annoys us, we can let a human being off, as well. Some of us hold on to things that people have done to us for a lifetime—not just a day or a month, but a lifetime. You have to understand that a lot of people are ignorant; they're not self-aware. Most people don't realize how hurtful they can be to another person.

It's like that stallion that bit me. I was in the stall with him one day while he was eating. I walked back behind the horse to clean up. He had hurt his hoof, and while I was trying to wash it, he stepped on me. Let me tell you, when a horse steps on you, it almost breaks your toe. You don't want to get him excited because he might step on you again. So you wait until he gets his foot off you and then you get out of there. But when you get out of there, you realize the horse didn't mean to hurt you. The horse didn't even know you were back there, he just stepped on you, thinking you were part of the floor.

The average person that steps on your feelings and hurts you is in the same situation. I've heard people on many occasions say, "How could she do this to me?" or, "How could he do that to me?" And the answer is simple. Just like that horse, they don't know what they're doing. Because probably if they knew they were hurting you, they wouldn't do it.

When you bring food out to a horse he's happy: If he knew that he was going to hurt the foot that brought the food, he wouldn't do it. Most people don't intend to hurt you, either. So that leaves us with the knowledge and wisdom that we must find a way to forgive them.

My grandfather had a lot of daughters, but there was one aunt I never knew; she died early. I'd hear them talking about her all the time. My grandfather had a mule, and at that time, a mule was a valuable asset. Not many people had tractors. It takes a long time to train a mule, but once you have, you've got a working piece of machinery. In those days, you depended on a mule whether you were working in the field—plowing or planting cotton—or you needed to make a trip to town in your wagon. So my mother's little sister was on the wagon one day out in the woods.

My grandfather raised his children to understand that if they screamed, there'd better be something wrong. He always told them, "If you hear someone hollering in the woods, it better be something to pardon." So when he heard screaming and hollering in the woods that day he came running. And when he did, he saw that the mule had run off with the wagon and that my aunt had fallen off and broken her neck. She died right there. He had nine daughters, but how did he feel about coming out there and seeing his baby dead? My mother never got over her sister's death. As a matter of fact, none of her relatives ever got over that incident.

My mother said her father was so upset he went to get his shotgun, and he was getting ready to blow out that mule's brains. He said, "Mule, I'm going to kill you right now. You killed my baby." And his uncle stepped in and said, "If you kill that animal, you're going to have to buy another one." He said, "If you kill that animal right now, you're going to have to go out and pay more and it's not even going to be as good as this one." He said, "An animal's dumb. It doesn't even know what it's done. It didn't intend to kill the baby; it didn't even know the baby was around." He said, "You can't kill the animal." My granddaddy was getting ready to blow his animal's brains out and his uncle talked him out of it. And the point of this story is that he was telling the truth. That animal was dumb. He didn't know what he was doing. Why kill that animal?

So I thought about some of the things some of us do to one another. The average person that hurts you doesn't know better. Men that walk away and devastate women, they just thought they were doing their thing; they didn't think about how their actions would affect the other person. Women that walk away and devastate men, they think, "I'm just doing my thing." Or a friend stops calling you. They usually don't think about what their actions will do any more than the horse that stepped on me. You have to suck it up and forgive them.

We bought this expensive door at home. I mean, we spent some bucks on that door. But one of our dogs came around to the back door, he wanted to come in, he started scratching. It's okay if he does it once. But the next day he wants to come in. No one's paying attention, and, then, after a couple of months I discovered that dog's dug a hole in that expensive door. Just like my grandpapa, I wanted to go out there and do something to that dog. But you know what? It wasn't the dog's fault. The dog just wanted to get to me. Just to be in there with me, that's all he wanted. So I found a way to keep that dog away from the door. I didn't destroy the dog. I didn't get rid of the dog. The dog wasn't thinking. He was just trying to get what he wanted and he didn't know enough to figure out another way to do it. We're human beings; we don't have that excuse. We've got to be smart.

We've got to learn to trust one another and forgive one another. If we can forgive an animal, we can forgive a human being. How many times should we forgive another person? We can't begin to count. We've all got to examine how much we truly love one another. We are responsible for one another. And the best thing we can do is try to always look for a way to forgive people. I can always find a way to forgive someone. If you can show me five different things one person has done to another, I can show you at least three different ways why they're not that bad. That's because we must seek ways to forgive one another.

THE
KISS
OF
DEATH

I HAVE preached all over the world. One thing I've noticed at funerals is how often people want to kiss the body. They practically snatch it out of the coffin. They say, "Let me give her a kiss." They ask, "All right if I kiss him?" They look to me for an answer. And I say, "Why are you asking me?" A kiss is something you give from your heart, not because some preacher with big arms gives you the nod. A kiss is how you express love and respect, not guilt and regret. That's why I call the type of kiss that comes too late "the kiss of death."

Treat people dearly while they are alive. I've seen sons

and daughters or granddaughters and grandsons come to see their mom or dad or grandma *after* they've died—to give them one last look and one last kiss. The unfortunate thing is they didn't consider doing that while the person was still alive—when their kisses and tears would have meant something. I've spoken at the funerals of people who have lived to be nearly one hundred years old and I know it had been decades since they received a single hug or a kiss from the ones who want to hang on to them now.

I'm reminded of all the gangster movies I've seen where some guy has done the head honcho wrong. Just before the boss has that guy killed, he grabs him and plants a big kiss right on the lips. That's the kiss of death. Because when the guy gets that kiss, he knows, "Boy, I'm dead now."

If I asked around about the people weeping and wailing over the body, I'm sure I would very often hear that these people weren't around much when the person who's gone was alive; they always had some excuse about why they couldn't come here or there, or why it was too much trouble to do this or that. They're carrying on for themselves. Their grief is made heavier because they'll never be able to make things right. On the other hand, if I were to ask about the people who come by the coffin and simply say, " 'Bye, darling, I love you," I'm sure I would hear something altogether different. These people didn't miss the chance to tell their loved ones how much they mattered while they were alive. Their grief is not compounded by guilt. All they need to say now is, "You mean so much to me. I'm not sure what I'm going to do without you. I wish I could have a few more years with you."

So don't wait until that person is lying dead in the ground. Then it's too late—way too late. We've got to make certain that we are giving those kisses to our loved ones while they are alive. And I don't mean just the physical act of hugging and kissing. I mean treating them like you love them by the way you live every day. Do as much for one another while the people you care about are alive. That's when the show is on.

FRIEND-
SHIP

IT'S THE easiest thing in the world to tell somebody, "I'm your friend," or, "We're friends." But to do the things that mark you as a true friend—not just a buddy to hang out with—that's as demanding as it gets. You have to be able to call on everything you've got when your friend calls on you.

If you really are going to be a friend, you've got to have a clear understanding of what friendship means. People often think of a friend as someone who helps you enjoy good times. But life is not just about good times: There are going to be some rough times in this world. A real friend is in your corner for the hard times as well as the high times.

By the time I left boxing the first time, I didn't have many friends. I had been so surly for so long, I had driven nearly everyone away—even my own mother didn't like being around me. It didn't matter that I had been heavy-weight champion of the world; now I was in a world of hurt. I was on my own and I was helpless: I didn't even know how to change a flat tire. That's when I realized what separates one guy from another is that one has a friend to help him out—to help him past his adversity—and the other guy is alone.

And there are a lot of people who fall. Sometimes they fall so hard and so far that nobody can get them. If only they'd had a friend to catch them just as they were lean-ing—caught them and supported them until they could find their balance—they never would have hit the ground. The ground can be depression or divorce or even the bank foreclosing on your house. You might think that the people who fall didn't know another soul, that they didn't have people in their lives who called themselves friends. But they did—or they thought they did—until they needed a hand. That's when they realized, "I can't just take my two kids to their home. I can't invite myself over to their place for din-ner. I can't show up at their apartment even though I have no place else to go." Sure, they had people they called up to say, "Let's get some coffee, let's go to a movie, let's take the kids to the park." But when it was time to fall, they looked around and there wasn't anyone there. So they had to fall hard, and they had to fall by themselves.

Friendship comes with responsibilities. If you're going to tell someone, "I'll be your friend, I'll always be there," you'd

Dick Van Dyke and I are having a staring contest on his comedy show in 1975. I won! After that, we took off our robes as though we were going to box, but we sat down and played a game of chess instead.

better be ready to shoulder those burdens. Because in the long run, if you don't, you're going to make whoever's leaning on you fall even harder. Falling hurts but it hurts even more when someone you thought you could depend on wasn't there for you.

You need a friend when bad luck strikes. And no one just slides along without ever bumping into some misfortune. Sometime something is going to happen that you don't have any control over. There are so many doors to walk through in life, you never know what's behind them—there's the door of loneliness, the door of unemployment, the door of sickness. A real friend cannot say, "Okay, you can be my friend, but if you happen to hit that particular door—that scary-looking one with the skull and crossbones on it—I'm done with our friendship."

That's why we have to look deep within ourselves and understand what really goes into a friendship. Spell it out for yourself. What if this person were to lose his head or lose his home or lose his money? Would you still be there? If you're able to accept those responsibilities, you can call yourself a friend. You need to be able to say honestly and without reservations, "I'm your friend because I love you, there's something special about you. No matter what happens to you, I'm going to be there."

It doesn't matter how much you have; what matters is what you're willing to give. There are people who own a fancy house in Los Angeles, a business apartment in New

York, and maybe a vacation home in Barbados. But when a friend needs a bed and a roof over their head, they think, "Well, I can't let him move into my house in Los Angeles. I need my business apartment in Manhattan. I can't let him stay at my vacation place. I don't know what to do, I don't know how to help him."

Sharing is the hardest thing for some people. They don't want anyone to be dependent on them. But you have to assume that your friends are going to need you—emotionally, physically, even financially—sooner or later. And if you've gotten to be too good to give of yourself and share what you've got, then you have to accept the fact that you don't really have friends.

Years ago, one of my aunts was taking care of my grandmother. She had brought my grandmother to live with her in San Francisco. But my grandmother just wasn't a city person. She came from the country where she had a one-room house without running water. That one room served as the bedroom, the kitchen, the bathroom, and everything else. And the roof leaked. My aunt's house, by contrast, had private bedrooms and bathrooms and every luxury. But my grandmother wanted to be in the country, she wanted her life back, she wanted to be *home*. She was afraid she was going to die in San Francisco. Finally she returned to East Texas. And the next year, everyone in the family who could, gave money to put running water in the house. The first time I got some money and I was able to contribute, it felt good.

But before long I realized we hadn't done nearly enough. I took a reporter by to visit my grandmother one day. We were sitting in the yard, and I said to the reporter, "This is my grandmother." Then I looked at her, and I thought, "This is *my* grandmother." That was the first time I really understood my obligation to take care of her. Not long after that, we decided to build her a brand-new home. For years, she had been afraid every time it rained—all that thunder and lightning frightened her. And for years, she would always say she was only going to live a couple more years. So we built the house underneath a tree she had planted when she was a young girl, and that tree sheltered her from the rain. The house had a little ramp for her wheelchair and her own bathroom and a king-size bed. Once after that, she looked at me and she said, "You know what? I bet I'm going to live about twenty more years now."

The point is, it had been easy for me to say "that lady," but once you say "*my* grandmother" or "*my* friend," you assume a responsibility for that person. That's what friendship is all about. Even after you put your friends away in the ground, the friendship goes on. Love is stronger than death. It doesn't die if they die. It doesn't die if they lose their looks. It doesn't die if something bad is written about that person in the newspaper. It comes with a strong obligation and you can't just decide to put it down because a person is down.

If someone gets sick—even if they lose their mind and

can't recognize you anymore—that should not affect your friendship. I've seen people who have had loved ones who were doing fine one day and the next day they called them strange names and told them, "Get out of my face, I don't want to have anything to do with you." That didn't do anything but strengthen the bond they had with that person. They might say, "Momma doesn't know me anymore," and laugh about it, but they didn't mean, "That's no longer my mother."

The gift of friendship is as great a gift as any you ever get in life. We have to hold on to that friendship, cling to it, and never let it go.

SAY SOMETHING NICE

THERE'S AN old expression that says if you can't say something nice about someone, you shouldn't say anything at all. That rule counts double when you're talking to people about their children.

If you ever marry someone who already has children, you might think, "I'm married to her now, I ought to tell her that her son has bad manners," or, "He's my husband, I should point out that his daughter can't read very well." Your husband or wife might even agree with you. They'll say, "Yeah, that's right." But that doesn't mean they wanted to hear those kinds of comments. Every time you criticize one of their children, it cuts deep. It doesn't matter whether it's true. Each negative thing you say leaves another scar on their heart. It doesn't matter how close you are to people—you could be their best friend or even *their* mother or father—they still don't want you to find fault with their kids no matter how old they are. Sometimes grown siblings say disparaging things about one another to their parents. They don't seem to understand they're just killing their old mother and father when they make remarks like, "He's no good." You can be sure that that momma and daddy have known what their son is like longer than anybody.

"Well," you say, "someone's got to tell them." Yes, and believe me, *someone* will. Just make sure it's not you. Any time you open your mouth to talk about someone else's child, make sure it's to pay them a compliment or at least to say something inoffensive.

People only want to hear the best about their children. That's because every mom and dad feels their child is an extension of themselves. So pointing out their kid's shortcomings—whether they're physical, emotional, or behavioral—hurts because it feels like it's a reflection on them and their success as a parent. As soon as you say something's wrong with that boy or girl, their mother or father starts a conversation inside their head that goes something like, "If only I were better at this or if only I had done that, my child wouldn't have this problem." It doesn't really matter what you say or that you meant well; what they hear is, "What's the matter with you? Couldn't you have done a better job?"

If you're a parent, you spend your life trying to correct

everything you feel is wrong with your kids; you're aware of even the tiniest flaws. And those you can't fix, you usually try to hide from others. So it's all the more painful when someone else sees what you tried so hard to conceal. Whatever it is, it seems like it's your fault. And you might think that if only you'd fixed it soon enough, no one would have noticed.

If you know for a fact that kids are doing something that could hurt them or hurt someone else, you have an obligation to say something to their parents. But folks who tell you bad news about your kids often don't have the best intentions. Sometimes, they tell you just to see how the information will affect you. As a father, one situation that really bothered me was the time a person I know made sure to tell me that one of my grown children had gotten a tattoo. What upset me was not that one of my kids had a tattoo. That child was an adult; it was a personal decision. But my child should have had the opportunity to tell me about it before someone else did.

I've noticed that nearly every loving parent wants the same basic things for their children: They want them to be successful—however they define that—and they want other people to love and accept their kids without conditions. I have ten kids. That's what I want for each one.

But especially when you've had a child by more than one mother, as I have, you find that that's not what always happens. Each mother loves her own child and wishes the other children well. In my family, I am the only one who loves all of them equally. I wish that weren't the case. I want somebody to love

In 1973, after I beat Joe Frazier in Kingston, Jamaica, to take the heavyweight title, I was given a welcome-home parade in Houston. For a lot of the kids, I was their first Houston hero.

every one of my kids. At home sometimes, I'll see two of my daughters sitting together while a third is excluded from the group. At school, there's always a teacher who seems to care for one of my kids more than another. Or there's a guy who falls in love with one daughter and barely says a word to another. Even in marriage, a woman pledges her love to only one son, for better or for worse. But I love every one of my children the same. Every night I go to sleep counting and praying for each of them.

For most of my adult life, I've given some of my income to colleges across the country for kids who run out of funds in school. Sometimes people tell me, "You better slow down." But I always say to myself, "You would not say that if the money were for your child."

This was a lesson I learned early. When I was a young man and into trouble in Houston, my mom asked my first boxing teacher and trainer in California, Doc Broadus, to help get me out of town. He sent me a plane ticket and paid for my room—just because my mom asked.

Years later, he told me that his wife had left him because she had kept saying, "You keep helping those no-good boys who never amount to anything; you need to send that money home." She was right; most of us had let him down. But that's when he said to me, "George, I could not put my family first after Mrs. Nancy asked me to help like that. I loved you all the same as my own children."

To this day, I am afraid to love any child less than I love my own kids.

LOVE AND MARRIAGE

EVER SINCE I can remember, I've been competing against someone. When I was just a toddler, I would dance to get my mom's attention or I'd run to be the first of my brothers and sisters to reach my dad. When I was older, I'd get on my bicycle, not just to ride for fun but to prove I was faster than the other boys in my neighborhood. I spent my whole life trying to outdo everyone else. Even winning the Olympic gold medal and the heavyweight championship belts weren't enough for me. Next, I was trying to be the most admired man on everyone's list.

My competitive streak was so consuming that it poisoned my marriages. I didn't try to be the best husband; instead, I tried to be better than my wife at everything. I felt that since I was the man in the relationship, I had to be the successful one. I had to win every disagreement. It was always "my" and "I" and "I did this" or "I did that." There was never any room for two.

It was a long time before I understood how much other people had helped me get where I am in life. Without six other children at home to help out, my mom never could have said to me, "Go, son, make something of your life," when I left Houston for the Job Corps at age sixteen. And only because there were so many there to take care of *her* could I leave without fearing for my mom's well-being. I could never have come to the doorstep of the Almighty without the love of my children in my heart. And there's no way I would have my dear children without the women who gave birth to them.

In each relationship, I counted only the material possessions I had given: homes, cars, and money. And that was *all* I'd ever given. But one day I looked at my wife, Joan, and realized that what she was giving me was so precious, it had no price tag: She was devoting herself to me and to our life together. She had adopted the modest ways of a preacher's wife, she had taken in all my kids, and she never boasted about her accomplishments. I came to understand that giving totally of yourself is the only true gift that matters between a husband and a wife.

I have been married five times, but I would have married five hundred times if that's what it took to get it right. I am so glad I now know what it's like to be truly married. I've found out that love is allowing yourself to be vulnerable, where I used to think that was just weakness. I realize now that the women who left me were trying to get me to say, "I love you," and mean it, instead of just giving them *things*. I've had to tell myself many times that while I can't go back and undo past hurt, I can make *this* marriage the best I can. Now, my wife is my role model. I've learned that she's often totally right and the fact that I'm her husband doesn't mean that I can always do things my way. She's the one who has taught me how to love and cherish.

When a man gets married he has to put down his baton, his running shoes, and his boxing gloves. All the competition has to stop. What's important is that the husband and wife cross the finish line together. Now, I try never to win at anything with my wife. Words like, "I got you," "I told you so," and "*my* child" have no place in a marriage. It's no longer enough for my wife to have all that I *own*, I want her to have all that I *have*: I want to give her all of *me*.

KEEPING LOVE ALIVE

MARRIAGE IS as natural as birds flying, but that doesn't mean it's always easy; even birds sometimes fly around in circles. I've been married five times, and one thing I've learned is that whether it's your first marriage or your fourth, most people tend to make the same mistakes.

What I know firsthand is that you can't have a true union unless you put your husband or wife above everything else. The first time I was married, in the early 1970s, I was building my boxing career, and I had only one goal in mind: becoming heavyweight champion. There was never a moment when I valued my marriage more than winning that title. You don't have to be a heavyweight contender to get your priorities mixed up. If you sit around all weekend watching sports on TV, you will probably have to start spending some of your time a little differently once you're married—unless that's something you both like to do together. I've noticed that people let all kinds of things get in the way of their relationship: They spend extra time at their job to make a good impression on their boss, when the person they should be impressing with their love is sitting at home. Or they let their friends and family members call the shots, forgetting that when you marry, your husband's or wife's wants and needs have to come first.

I also know you can spoil your relationship by putting too many burdens on it. Your husband or wife cannot solve all of your problems or fulfill every one of your needs. Two of the best friends in the world can become enemies simply by thinking they can take that same relationship into their marriage. To this day, I have friends I tell all my problems to. Before I married my wife, she was one of them. I could show my friends photos of my past life and we all could laugh. But make no mistake, when folks are married, the door has to close forever on your previous relationships. Even if you used to talk about your former girlfriends or boyfriends, all of that must stop when you get married. Your spouse doesn't want to keep dragging one foot back into the past. When you're married, you can even become jealous of the dead. Your husband or your wife will say, "Why do you keep bringing up his or her name when we're working so hard to build our own successful relationship?"

Talk business on your job site; talk about the past with your friends. Husbands and wives have to learn to talk love all the days of their life.

Marriage means accepting people for who they are— not trying to mold them into what you hope they'll become. Twice, I married women who thought they were signing on for an extravagant lifestyle. I was just as much at fault. I said "I do" to a woman whose favorite pastime was shopping, and I expected her to change her ways.

Building a life for two also means accepting your spouse's children with an open heart. Children from previous relationships are not "previous" children; they are there forever: Mothers' and fathers' hearts are tied to their children until death. A parent might throw up his or her hands a hundred times over something one of the kids has done but will never forgive a spouse who says, "I give up."

What I've learned to do is let every day be like the first day you fell in love. It's about paying attention to the little things and trying to put your best self forward, not just to others—your boss and your best friend and your neighbor—but to the one you've pledged your life to. That's not *always* possible—in love, there will be many things to come up: bills and sickness and disagreements. But none of that changes the fact that you came together to love, honor, and cherish each other to the end. When people say, "I do," something special happens that can only happen with marriage: Two become one—one body, one heart, and one in love. When you're married, it's time to build on what you have together. If you take a person to have and to hold, in sickness, in health, for better for worse, there will be no problems you can't resolve.

REINVENTING MARRIAGE

MY WIFE, Joan, is much younger than I am, and she grew up on an island in the Caribbean. So when I married her years ago, I had to teach her some basic skills for living in this country, like how to drive and where and what to shop for. She put her trust in me. But it wasn't long before my telling her what to do became a part of our daily life. It seems like I was always saying, "You better do this," or, "You better do that."

I really thought that after all my previous marriages I had finally found the perfect mate. She seemed so willing to do as I asked her. Then one day she stopped me and asked to talk. She said, "George, I have to tell you this: My father is dead and I miss him all the time, but he raised me. My mom told me years ago how to be a woman. I am an adult; I am not a child. I want you to respect me." What she said broke my heart because she was right. For a few years, I had been some big guy just pushing his weight around in my marriage like I did in the ring.

The realization that I had underestimated my wife devastated me because I loved her so. It had never occurred to me that while I was putting so much effort into bringing up my daughters to be independent-minded young women, I had overlooked my wife's need to have the same freedom. Because her experiences growing up in Saint Lucia were so different from the life we were living in Texas, I had mistaken those differences and what she needed to learn to live in the United States to mean that she needed to be shaped from scratch. I treated her as though I was always right and she didn't know how to handle herself without my instructions. But it turns out that *I* was the one who had much to learn. And my ignorance had led me to treat her without the respect she deserved. I asked her, "Please tell me what to do." All she said was, "George, just treat me the way you like to be treated." That really got me because I have never wanted anyone telling me what to do.

Marriage is a tricky equation. Two people come together to share one life, but they must still have the room to think and act as adults and as individuals. That conversation changed the way I thought about mature relationships. From that moment on, I realized that in marriage there are no bosses, only equal partners. My wife had only to speak up to bring about a change in my behavior, but there are so many people I see every day who have to find tremendous courage, strength, or faith to tell their husband or wife, "Treat me better now; not later, but today."

I tell my church members all the time: "Give your spouse freedom, not a divorce." Yet many people are afraid to let their husband or wife take ownership of themselves—afraid that if they do, they will somehow get away. I've found that's the way to keep a relationship strong over time. You have to trust love.

THE ONLY SIDES KIDS SHOULD HAVE TO CHOOSE ARE IN SPORTS

IN OUR society, so many couples end up getting divorced that splitting up can seem nearly as natural as getting married. But believe me, when two people decide to divorce, it is far from simple. For one thing, most people have a hard time admitting they might have failed. It's much easier to blame the other person for all the things that went wrong in the mar-

95

riage. That's the reason why some people go on and on saying negative things about their ex-husbands or ex-wives.

It's even more difficult when kids are caught in the middle between their mom and dad. Maybe they spend weekdays with one parent and weekends with the other. Whatever the arrangement, too often what happens is that when they tell their dad about something they did with their mom, he says something rude about that child's mother. Or they tell their mom something they did with their dad, and she says something insulting about him.

When it comes to children, parents have to be on the same side. It's hard enough for adults to know what to do when two of their friends split up—whether they can maintain a separate relationship with both members of the couple or whether they have to choose which one to keep up a friendship with. But children are not equipped to handle this burden, especially when it concerns the two people whom they probably love most. About the only situation I can think of where it's okay for children to pick who to root for is in sports.

I won't lie: There was a time when I loved to complain about the mother of one of my children. I blamed her for everything, from my son's bad grades to his unruly behavior. But one day, while he was living with me and going to school in Houston, I got a call from his grandmother in California. She said that her daughter, who had been sick with cancer, had died. I knew it was my responsibility to tell my son about his mom's death. As hard as that task was, I recognized that my past behavior made delivering the news even harder for both of us.

It still makes me cry to think about it now. For years, I had spoken negatively about his mom, and now I had to persuade my boy that I understood the overwhelming sadness he felt over her death. Oh, the hurt in my son! And all I could really do was to hope with all my heart that he had forgotten the comments I had made about his mother years earlier. I must have sent five thousand dollars in flowers for her funeral. But what I wished most is that I could have said kinder things about her and done better for her while she was alive.

I had not understood until then that my son loved his mother and me equally. Maybe he loved her even more. After all, he turned round and round in her body until it was time for him to come into this world. For years I thought my dear mom, who passed away a few years ago, was the only beloved mother in the world. But that day, I realized that my son had had the same blessing I had: He loved his mother, just as I loved mine. Thank God I figured it out before it was too late for me to change my behavior with my other children.

Sometimes kids are more mature than their parents. They know that they have to put their best foot forward with both their mom and their dad. But you shouldn't put your kids in the position of having to be a grown-up before they're ready. It's not their job to make peace or carry messages between you and your spouse. No matter how tense things are between you and your ex, you're the grown-up. It's your job to set the good example.

WHAT'S IN A NAME?

WHEN I was twenty-five years old, a couple of months after I lost the heavyweight title to Muhammad Ali in Africa in 1974, I was shocked to learn that my biological father was not J. D. Foreman, the man who raised me. I thought losing that fight was tough, but I think this second punch hit me even harder. Even though I met my natural father a few times before he died, I didn't get a chance to really get to know him—to study how he walked or behaved or to see if I had inherited any of his habits.

People often ask me why I gave each of my five boys my name: George Edward Foreman (some of my daughters have George as part of their names, too). They joke that I was too lazy to come up with something else, so I went for the name closest at hand, or that my ego must be *really huge*. But the truth is that after I found out I didn't have the roots I thought I had, I made a decision: I would plant some for my children that they could never lose. I wanted my kids to have a foundation that nobody could ever take from them—something they and their children and even their children's children could depend on if they ever felt disconnected from their family or their past.

Don't worry! We don't all come running whenever anyone calls out the name George; each of my sons goes by his own nickname. Because as much as I want them to understand exactly where they came from, it's just as important that they're recognized and treated as individuals.

My oldest son, born while I was still in Africa, is called Little George. The second boy goes by the name Monk, short for monkey, the same nickname my brothers and sisters gave me as a term of endearment when I was little more than a toddler and that the kids on the streets continued to call me as I grew up. Around the time my third son was born, my mother had started telling me stories of my grandfather Will Nelson and how she had seen so many of his ways in me. She said that he would work himself down to the ground before he would ask someone for help. That's when it occurred to me that you could pick up bad traits as well as good ones from your parents and grandparents. When I learned this, I changed my ways and nicknamed my third son as a reminder to both of us to always make sure you go your own way in life. As soon as he was born, I called him Big Wheel, my granddad's nickname. My fourth son seemed courageous, like David in the Bible, so I called him Red: The book of One Samuel describes David as "ruddy, with bright eyes." We call our youngest son Joe after my wife's dad, Joseph, who died when my wife was a teenager. Her dad could do so many things with his hands.

Even if they were all called the same thing, it's more than their names that set my kids apart. All children need attention and want answers, but each one is different.

I'm sitting on the front steps of our house in Kingwood, Texas, in 1994, with some of my children *(left to right)*: George IV, nicknamed "Big Wheel," after my grandfather; my youngest daughter, Leola; and George V, a.k.a. "Red."

Part of being a good parent is to recognize who your kids actually *are*, not who you *want* them to be. Parenting is not one size fits all. The strategy that works for one child doesn't work for all of them. And it's your job to match your parenting to the child, not the other way around. You never want your children to think, "Dad must have gotten me confused with one of my brothers or sisters. He must think he's talking to someone else." You can never let that happen. One slip, and you are no longer a source of trusted information for them.

Believe me, as a father of ten, keeping track of my children's distinct personalities can be pretty daunting. I try to go back in my mind to the day each of them was born,

because who they are now is almost exactly the same as who they were the day they came into this world. Of course people go through different phases, but I believe your temperament is pretty much locked in from the start. One of my children was the happiest baby I could ever imagine. Where a lot of infants wake up wailing, he started out each day laughing. I loved to watch his head moving this way and that as he followed the mobile that dangled above his crib. These days, he's a straight-up, no-nonsense guy. Like me, he loves music, jazz as well as classical, and that range tells me a lot about him. He takes it all in. He responds best when I give him concrete, detailed instructions, but he doesn't like it when I give him examples. With another, the advice is best when it's delivered in a soft, sweet tone and kept short. Some of my children don't need to be told what to do at all; they just need love and a regular phone call. One child hears me best when I ground my advice in stories about her mom and me; another likes to have me sing a song. One child can't stand to be teased, especially about girls. And then there's the one who *I* cannot stand to discipline!

Can you believe I have to keep this all in my head, with all the punches I got in boxing (smile)? It's true.

LOVE YOUR KIDS

I'VE FOUND that children generally reflect the attitudes and beliefs of their parents. When you meet kids who are happy and show kindness and compassion toward other people, it's usually because that's how their mom and dad behave. But you can meet kids who do nothing but whine and complain about how the world treats them, and their hard-working parents have no idea where their children picked that attitude up. Sometimes the bad attitude doesn't come from their parents; it comes from other people. You never know when some kids are being told at school that they're no good or that they can't do this or that. That's why what parents say can make a difference.

You might say, "Well I don't have any kids." Maybe not,

but you can still have a strong influence on children, even if they're not yours. Kids are always looking for role models. You can pop in and read them a story or coach their sports team or just spend a little time with them. And believe me, most parents will be grateful to anyone who impresses their kids in a positive way.

Children listen to the messages they get from adults more than you might think. You might feel sometimes when you're talking to them that nothing is getting through; that you're just speaking into a black hole. This can be especially true as they get older. But whether or not they acknowledge what you say, kids hear you, so never shy away from trying to teach them right from wrong. If you give up, all you're doing is leaving a vacuum for someone else—whether it's a friend or a TV show—to fill. You might be surprised to know who they really listen to. And you always want to get first dibs.

I believe *how* you teach your kids life's lessons is as important as *what* you teach them. I was watching a horse race on television the other day. The horses were running, and one jockey in particular seemed to know that his horse was not giving its all. So about halfway around the track, he whipped it, and that horse sped up into another gear. The average person watching would probably have thought the horse was running as hard as it could. But that jockey knew better; he'd been working with it. Soon they got around to the home stretch and the jockey picked up the whip again and just *showed* it to the horse and that horse took off and crossed the finish line and won all the money.

You can't beat good sense or obedience into your kids. You've got to love kids into another gear. You've got to love your kids no matter what. I've noticed that some parents use criticism like a whip. All they do is tell their kids how bad they are, how disappointing they are, that they'll never amount to anything. If you tell your children they're stupid and clumsy, that's what they'll believe. If you praise them for the efforts they make in school or in sports, they'll continue to try. You have to whisper words to your children you hope will protect them, words they can repeat to themselves and that are going to help them get somewhere good in life. Loving them and whispering the right words can help your kids make it across the finish line.

That's what my mother did for me when I was growing up. I would always strike out at people or things that made me angry or frustrated, and she constantly reminded me, "Son, you've got to stop losing your temper. Momma doesn't want you fighting." She would say, "It's better to hear, 'There he goes,' than, 'There he lays.'" She kept telling me that over and over. For it to become part of me, she must have started saying it when I was maybe three years old.

And there came a time when that message stood me in good stead. When I was a teenager, there was a guy in the neighborhood, Hilton Murdoch, who just did not like my best buddy. He liked me well enough and he respected me, but for some reason, he didn't take to my friend. One day the two of them were in the park and Murdoch said, "Hey, you think you're so tough. You want to box?" My buddy knew he could whip him, so he said, "Sure." But before he even got the first punch in, this guy Murdoch reached in his pocket and pulled out some brass knuckles and hit him. Blood went everywhere, and my friend got out of there as fast as he could. There was no telling what else Murdoch was planning to do to him. It was a blessing that's all he managed, because he was known as the worst kind of street fighter. He worked with a buddy, a guy named Ickyboo, who would come up from behind you and hit you in the head with a stick. So when my friend came to me and said, "Man, look what old Murdoch did," I said, "I'm going to find him."

I walked the neighborhood all that day, willing to take any chances to get him for what he'd done to my pal. Evidently, though, he got the word I was looking for him and he hid. It got to be nightfall and I still hadn't found him. By that time, my buddy had gone home to clean himself up, to put some ice on his eye. I was out in the yard playing some music and dancing, when out of the dark I saw the shadow of a hat. Murdoch always wore this hat. I saw the shadow and before I could even think, he was practically upon me, with Ickyboo right behind him. I looked down and saw that Murdoch was holding a knife that curved like a hook. It was a carpet knife. He eased up to me and said,

"I heard you were looking for me, man." I froze, thinking about how I was going to hit him, what I was going to do to him. And he said, "Are you looking for me, man?" All of a sudden I heard my mother's voice in my head: "It's better to have it said, 'There he goes,' than, 'There he lays.'" I just shrugged and said, "No man, I wasn't looking for you." My answer surprised even me. When I said that, he closed up his knife and his friend stepped back and they disappeared into the dark. This fellow Murdoch knew he'd backed me into a corner, and for a long time after that, I was embarrassed at how I had responded. But now I believe if I hadn't heard my mother whispering her wisdom in my head, I wouldn't have lived to see another day. To this day, I believe my mother saved my life.

LET YOUR KIDS BE KIDS

MY DEAR mom used to tell me with such pride how much she loved school when she was growing up. Although she didn't get far in her education, she was a great speller all her life; the bigger a word was, the easier it seemed for her.

One day when I asked her why she didn't have a high-school education, she told me, "Papa made us work." Her father was a poor sharecropper who depended on his eight daughters to help him out in the fields, even when they were supposed to be in school. "This will be the last time," my grandfather would say each time farming cut their school year short. But the next year would come around, and it would be just the same: His girls would have to put their books aside so they could plant and pick cotton.

My mother didn't always leave school willingly. Once she and one of my aunts begged my grandmother, "Momma, please let us go to school this week." My mom told me that was one of the few times her mother, who was nearly always sick, stood up to her husband, and said, "Will, let them go this week." My grandfather didn't say one word back to her about it, and they got to go back to school.

I am sure my grandfather did the best he could, but I believe my mother and aunts should never have been faced with so much adversity early in life. I've always felt that every child should have a chance to be happy and to feel safe and secure—to skip and play without worrying and to climb into bed at night with a hug. They need to know that the next day is going to follow in pretty much the same way. For parents, providing that sort of emotional and physical stability can take a real effort.

In spite of the way my mother was raised, when she grew up and had seven kids of her own, she did everything she could to give us that kind of secure childhood. Even though she worked two jobs for years, I never heard her complain about her life. She didn't burden us with her problems; she greeted us with a smile every day when she came home. She often told stories that started out something like, "Son, when they bombed Pearl Harbor," as though wartime had defined her life experience as a young woman. But it wasn't until I was older that I found out how truly stressful and full of sacrifices that time had really been. Even as little as we had to get along on, she shielded us from a lot of life's ugliness.

As a father, I've always tried to give my own kids the room to be children as long as possible. Once I saw my daughter Natalie carrying her little sister on her side as we were getting into the car. I asked her, "Why are you carrying the baby?" She said, "Mom told me to." I said to her—in front of my wife—"If you would like to play with the baby, she's your sister, you can do that all you want. But taking care of her will never be your duty. Your mom and I love you, and we had you because we wanted children. We didn't have any of you so you could take care of us or your brothers and sisters or to share our responsibilities. So darling," I said to Natalie, "keep those babies off your hip."

I have been pained by all the unrest and hatred that are happening in the world, but I don't go into that with my kids. That's because I never want to call "time's up" too soon on their childhoods. Let them run and sing as long as they can. The serious side of life will be waiting for them soon enough.

TELL YOUR CHILDREN THE TRUTH

TOO MANY parents hide the truth from their kids. Don't let your children grow up embracing lies, because the lies you tell them when they're young can come back around to trip them when they grow up. Don't give them facts of life that don't exist. You might have heard guys say, "When I get married, I've got to marry a virgin." That's because they have been taught to believe that's what their mother and father did, that that's the only respectable thing to do. Then they find out later that when their mother married their daddy, she was twenty miles from being a virgin. Come clean with your kids so they can come clean with their own lives.

Too many times I've heard men say, "I want a woman just like my mom." But they don't know everything there is to know about their mom. Maybe their mother hasn't come clean with them. Or I've heard women say, "I've got to marry a man just like my dad." But their dad may not have been anything until their mother found him and made something out of him. When a guy starts getting gray hair or no hair, people automatically start thinking he's wise and distinguished. You never know how he behaved when he was younger. He could have been a terror and his wife might have had to put up with a lot of stuff. Come clean with your kids, because if you don't, they might end up turning their backs on a potential mate who might make them happy.

I'm not saying you need to tell your children what they're not ready to hear or aren't able to handle. When little kids ask where babies come from, you don't have to give them all the details; you can just say something simple like, "That's what happens when moms and dads love each other." But at some point when they're older, you've got to tell them straight up.

It's the same with bad habits you had that you don't want them to take up. Early on, you can say, "I don't want

112

you to smoke. It's bad for you." Later, you can tell them you used to smoke and you don't want them to start because you know how it makes you feel and what a vicious habit it is to break. It's up to you as a parent to gauge when and what they're ready to take in. In the same way kids won't tell you that their shoes are too tight, as a parent, you have to pay attention, to metaphorically try the shoes on your own feet to see if they've outgrown them. It's the same with advice: There is a time when frankness has to be moved up a size.

Recently, one of my sons who is nineteen years old had a heart-to-heart talk with me about love and marriage. He wanted to know what to look for in a woman, how you decide to give your love, how to tell if she is a good woman. He was being too serious to lie to. So I told him all I could about love and picking a wife someday. My son thinks his grandma (my mom) was the best woman to walk the earth. But I said, "Son, I want you to know something: Grandma had children and they were not all by the same man." He couldn't believe what I was telling him. He said, "Why are you telling me this?" I said, "I want you to know that if you love someone, you cannot have a preconception of what she is or of her past. It doesn't matter who Mom and Dad want you to marry but who you want. You are free to love who you want!" I had to let him know. His feet were big enough.

I was in a similar situation years ago when some of my

113

daughters were younger. I told them, "You have been dating this guy a year; if there is no real commitment now, there never will be." But what was I to do after that when they thought they had a real commitment from a young guy and they were thinking they had done the right thing even when they knew marriage was a bad decision? Because the engagement was made, because of the advice I gave them, they plodded ahead. I had to be the one to step up and look for an opening to rework my own advice. "You know," I told them, "I was engaged once; trying to be a good guy and to save this girl's name. Even though I knew I would never be happy or make her happy, I wanted to make everybody else happy. But finally I told my family and my friends, 'I changed my mind.' Sure there were hurt feelings and anger, but I look back and we all are happy because of it." I had to know when my children were stuck in the wrong size advice and move it up a notch.

WHEN LIFE KNOCKS YOU DOWN

LOVING YOUR children is the number-one job of any mom or dad. But no matter how much love and support you give your kids, the real world is still going to throw punches at them. As a parent, you can't always protect your kids from getting hurt, but what you can do is prepare them to pick themselves up. Parents have to impress upon kids early that they can't allow the disappointment and rejection that are inevitably part of this life to shake their belief in themselves.

I learned this the hard way. I fell in love with a girl from Houston I'd been courting since I was about fifteen years old. Finally, when I was seventeen and in the Job Corps, she wrote me a "Dear John" letter. I went around the whole dormitory and showed everyone the letter. And I would say over and over, "I loved this girl and I bought her a ring; I even got a job to pay for the ring, and look what she's done: She has gotten another boyfriend." I said, "I'll show her: One day, I'm going to be famous and she'll want me back."

That's exactly what I did. I became an Olympic Gold medalist. I was on television; I even went on *The Dating Game*. And I became a professional boxer. I was about to turn twenty, and I thought I had it all. So I rented a room at a fancy hotel in Houston and I called this girl up and told her I was downtown. I said, "I want you to come have dinner with me; there's something I want to talk to you about." I was going to ask her to marry me. She said, "That won't be possible, my fiancé will be in town." I said, "That's it. I'm not taking any more of this. I have known you for years. I've written you, I've called you, I've even bought you a ring. I've told you I love you, and I've respected you. I was going to give you my life. But I'm done. You will never have anyone who loves you like I love you but I'm through." And I hung up the phone.

> I'm showing off my title belt and a muscle or two after winning the heavyweight title in 1994, the oldest man ever to do so.

But when I slammed the receiver back in the cradle, I was a different person. I let this one incident shape how I looked at relationships with women. I let myself be shaped by rejection.

A couple of weeks later I was in Houston again, and a friend told me, "Look, there's this wonderful girl, she goes to Texas Women's College in Denton, Texas. She's a lovely girl and she's always wanted to meet you." So she stopped by. And when she drove up, I looked through the hotel window and saw the prettiest girl I'd ever seen in my life. She liked me to a fare-thee-well. But it didn't matter. I had become a cruel boy without any good intentions. The disappointment had shaped me

My trainer, Dick Sadler, is taking my glove off after a sparring session, getting me ready for the big Ali match in 1974 in Zaire.

into someone I didn't want to be because my mother and dad had never told me a fundamental truth about life: You may like people, you may care a lot about a girl or a guy, but that has nothing to do with whether they'll feel the same way back. You've got to let that go and believe in yourself and find someone who cares about you in return.

In those days, there was always something sad about the girls who liked me—like a sad, lonesome song. I guess they were sad because they liked me. So I kept messing with women who didn't care for me at all. You've got to choose people who love you and forget about those who don't or, like me, you'll end up for years fighting against it. I must

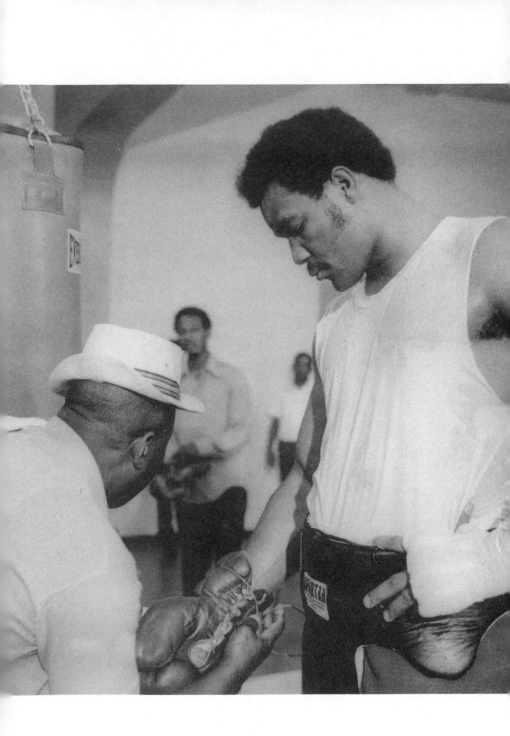

have been a thirty-year-old man and I still thought there was something lacking in me. I still hadn't gotten over that girl turning me down. I had let myself be defined by rejection. Now I know that being angry and resentful of someone is like letting them live rent-free in your head.

I allowed someone else's bad behavior to affect me, not just in this one incident: I allowed this rejection to shape my reactions to women for years and years to come. You have to make it clear to your kids that life is going to beat you up a little bit but you've got to be resilient.

I let one thing rob me of years of happiness. Ultimately, I wound up with a woman I love and a good, strong marriage. But think how much heartache I would have saved myself and others if I had picked myself up off the canvas; if I had been able to get past this.

LETTING GO

AS A FATHER of ten kids, I've been raising children nearly my whole adult life. What I've found is that there's no tougher part of parenting than stepping back to let kids live a life of their own. I got so used to having my children depend on me that I was fooled into thinking they'd need me in the same way when they were twenty as they did when they were twelve.

I had my awakening the day my fourth daughter, Natalie, who had been elected head of the student council at prep school, gave a speech at her graduation.

She spoke of how lonely she had been in her first days at a new school in Connecticut and of the hours she'd spent staring out the window trying to figure out why she was there, so far from her family in Texas. That's when she found out who she was, she said. Until then, she had always been the person her parents wanted her to be. Although her loneliness didn't

121

go away, she told the audience that another, stronger purpose had been born: She was determined to carve out a life for herself. And while her tears didn't stop immediately, she cried over the new realization that she had always tried to live up to other people's expectations, never stopping to think about what *she* valued and *needed* and wanted for herself.

Her words that day made *me* cry. Until I heard her speak, I had no idea she had been through such a hard time when she first left home. I kept asking myself, "How could she have gotten through that time alone?"

Life magazine ran this photo after I recaptured the title in 1994. The publication wanted to show how many differences there are in athletes.

But that's not the only thing that made me weep. I understood that she had made a life for herself that wasn't about me; that my job of helping put her on the right track in life was basically finished. For the first time, I had to look at my child as an independent woman—one who had a future that belonged to her separately from me and what I might want. I had to understand that the choices that she would make in her new life have nothing to do with my love for her. Despite my tears, I was happy and proud because she had made it on her own without any help from her mom or me. "I want to be a doctor for the children who will be sick in my generation," she told me. "That means I'll have to have the best education possible."

That day, as I listened to all Natalie had to say, my mind

jumped back to the time I owned a Doberman puppy in the 1970s. When I took my pup in for her six-month checkup, the vet told me, "This puppy looks and acts about the same now as she will when she's fully grown; she won't change much after this. She'll fill out, but you'll continue to see the same dog you have right now."

When I looked at my daughter, I thought, "She has become a young woman. She has everything she needs to live a successful life but her independence." The only things left for my wife and me to do were to give her guidance when she asks for it and to pay for her college education. I thought, "How can we do this without trying to possess her?"

I had trained my old Doberman pup so that when she sat, I gave her a treat; when she rolled over, she got another treat. The deal was: No trick, no treat.

I was determined to let my child be a human being with no strings attached—no jumping for treats. This is a hard move to make, letting your kids go. But it's a pleasure for me to know that this is one of the most important lessons I will pass on to each one of my children when they're ready. It was the same for my mom and me years back when I left Houston to become a boxer. She didn't urge me to go to California because she wanted to see me go; she did so because she realized that leaving offered me the best chance to live a full, successful life as an adult. One day, my kids, too, will learn from me and let *their* kids go out into the world.

IF YOU ENJOYED
THIS BOOK...

I INVITE YOU to visit with me online at www.GeorgeForeman.com. Discover the most important things as we share recipes for success in all areas of life. Join my community discussions on family, friends, and making your life as meaningful as possible. Or just check out what's new at the Ranch. See what I have been up to lately, and a whole bunch of new things I like. Stop by www.GeorgeForeman.com anytime, and explore all aspects of living, with a winning attitude.

PHOTO CREDITS